DAILY

Gratitude & Intention

JOURNAL

By

Heather Doyle Fraser

Introduction

Do you feel abundant every morning when you awake and as you fall asleep at night? Do you experience abundance coming into your life on a daily basis? If you answered "yes" to these questions then this is the journal for you, and if you answered "no" to these questions then this is also the journal for you!

In my work as a transformational life coach with clients, I have noticed something about the people who experience an overall feeling of abundance - they show and express gratitude daily, and they make decisions based on this gratitude and state of abundance. It shapes their reality and their place in the world. For those who do not *formally* practice being grateful on a daily basis, it is much harder for them to sense and access that state of abundance because these people are making decisions and experience the world from a place of lack.

So, how do those of us who don't generally feel abundant move to that place of gratitude? PRACTICE. That's right, practice. The good news is that research shows it only takes 21 days to build a habit - just three weeks; the key, though, is making the practice so simple that it can be consistently repeated until it becomes part of the fabric of your daily life.

There are many ways that you could go about building this practice, but there is one way that I have found to be more effective than others for most people. The strategy I use with my clients is to begin a Gratitude and Intention Journal. Sometimes, though, the idea of a blank page staring at you in the morning is just paralyzing, so I give people a SIMPLE format:

Gratitudes: Today, I am grateful for...

1.

2.

3.

Intention: Today, my intention is ...

Committed Action: Today, the actions I will take to manifest my goals, dreams, and intentions are ...

As you can see, I ask people to write down three different things for which they are grateful everyday. These can be anything: you could be grateful for the place you live, for your job, for your partner, for your independence, for the sun shining on your face, for the sound of the rain on your roof, or the smell of steaming, hot coffee as it rushes towards you from the kitchen in the morning. You could be grateful for your friendships, your children, your pets, your solitude, your creativity, your discipline or your carefree attitude. You could deeply appreciate the beauty around you found in a flower or the changing seasons or the fragrance of fresh cut grass or a home-cooked meal. You can show your gratitude for anything!

Next, what do you want to make of your day? What intentions do you want to set in motion to create that abundant reality. Write an intention for each day, and then write down one or more committed actions you will take to make those intentions and dreams a reality and bring you to that state of abundance. It is that simple.

You will notice that there are 365 entry opportunities in this journal. Write in this journal every day - no exceptions. Start your daily practice today and experience your abundant life!

About the Author

Heather Doyle Fraser is a Transformational Life Coach and founder/owner of Beyond Change, LLC. As a coach, Heather works with highly successful people who feel blocked, stuck or lost in one or more areas of their lives. She holds the space for her clients as they move toward and acknowledge their inherent greatness while achieving their goals and vision for an extraordinary life. Heather's mission is to inspire joy and transformation and give people the knowledge, skills, and strategies to live their most authentic and fulfilled lives.

If you would like to learn more about coaching or contact Heather, please visit her website at www.beyondchangecoach.com or connect with her on Facebook or Twitter @hdoylefraser.

Gratitudes

Intentions

Committed Actions

An Abundant Life

Date: 6/4/16

Gratitudes: Today, I am grateful for...

1. I am blessed with a loving family.

2. I have wonderful, caring friends.

3. I have a beautiful place to live.

Intention: Today, my intention is...

Get started sorting in the basement.
Develop a plan of action for packing
and getting rid of "things.

Committed Action: Today, the actions I will take to manifest my goals, dreams, and intentions are...

1) Separate keep from get rid of in basement
2) Put photos away to clean table

Date: 6/5/16

Gratitudes: Today, I am grateful for...

1. Early morning light

2. Birds of all kinds and their songs

3. Being able to meet Scott and Sam for lunch / seeing Fitz.

Intention: Today, my intention is...

Enjoy seeing Britt, Scott, Sam and Fitz and be at ease and relaxed,

Committed Action: Today, the actions I will take to manifest my goals, dreams, and intentions are...

Smile
Give compliments

Date:

Gratitudes: Today, I am grateful for...

1.

2.

3.

Intention: Today, my intention is...

Committed Action: Today, the actions I will take to manifest my goals, dreams, and intentions are...

Date:

Gratitudes: Today, I am grateful for...

1.

2.

3.

Intention: Today, my intention is...

Committed Action: Today, the actions I will take to manifest my goals, dreams, and intentions are...

Date:

Gratitudes: Today, I am grateful for...

1.

2.

3.

Intention: Today, my intention is...

Committed Action: Today, the actions I will take to manifest my goals, dreams, and intentions are...

Date:

Gratitudes: Today, I am grateful for...

1.

2.

3.

Intention: Today, my intention is...

Committed Action: Today, the actions I will take to manifest my goals, dreams, and intentions are...

Date:

Gratitudes: Today, I am grateful for...

1.

2.

3.

Intention: Today, my intention is...

Committed Action: Today, the actions I will take to manifest my goals, dreams, and intentions are...

Date:

Gratitudes: Today, I am grateful for...

1.

2.

3.

Intention: Today, my intention is...

Committed Action: Today, the actions I will take to manifest my goals, dreams, and intentions are...

Date:

Gratitudes: Today, I am grateful for...

1.

2.

3.

Intention: Today, my intention is...

Committed Action: Today, the actions I will take to manifest my goals, dreams, and intentions are...

Date:

Gratitudes: Today, I am grateful for...

1.

2.

3.

Intention: Today, my intention is...

Committed Action: Today, the actions I will take to manifest my goals, dreams, and intentions are...

Date:

Gratitudes: Today, I am grateful for...

1.

2.

3.

Intention: Today, my intention is...

Committed Action: Today, the actions I will take to manifest my goals, dreams, and intentions are...

Date:

Gratitudes: Today, I am grateful for...

1.

2.

3.

Intention: Today, my intention is...

Committed Action: Today, the actions I will take to manifest my goals, dreams, and intentions are...

Date:

Gratitudes: Today, I am grateful for...

1.

2.

3.

Intention: Today, my intention is...

Committed Action: Today, the actions I will take to manifest my goals, dreams, and intentions are...

Date:

Gratitudes: Today, I am grateful for...

1.

2.

3.

Intention: Today, my intention is...

Committed Action: Today, the actions I will take to manifest my goals, dreams, and intentions are...

Date:

Gratitudes: Today, I am grateful for...

1.

2.

3.

Intention: Today, my intention is...

Committed Action: Today, the actions I will take to manifest my goals, dreams, and intentions are...

Date:

Gratitudes: Today, I am grateful for...

1.

2.

3.

Intention: Today, my intention is...

Committed Action: Today, the actions I will take to manifest my goals, dreams, and intentions are...

Date:

Gratitudes: Today, I am grateful for...

1.

2.

3.

Intention: Today, my intention is...

Committed Action: Today, the actions I will take to manifest my goals, dreams, and intentions are...

Date:

Gratitudes: Today, I am grateful for...

1.

2.

3.

Intention: Today, my intention is...

Committed Action: Today, the actions I will take to manifest my goals, dreams, and intentions are...

Date:

Gratitudes: Today, I am grateful for...

1.

2.

3.

Intention: Today, my intention is...

Committed Action: Today, the actions I will take to manifest my goals, dreams, and intentions are...

Date:

Gratitudes: Today, I am grateful for...

1.

2.

3.

Intention: Today, my intention is...

Committed Action: Today, the actions I will take to manifest my goals, dreams, and intentions are...

Date:

Gratitudes: Today, I am grateful for...

1.

2.

3.

Intention: Today, my intention is...

Committed Action: Today, the actions I will take to manifest my goals, dreams, and intentions are...

Date:

Gratitudes: Today, I am grateful for...

1.

2.

3.

Intention: Today, my intention is...

Committed Action: Today, the actions I will take to manifest my goals, dreams, and intentions are...

Date:

Gratitudes: Today, I am grateful for...

1.

2.

3.

Intention: Today, my intention is...

Committed Action: Today, the actions I will take to manifest my goals, dreams, and intentions are...

Date:

Gratitudes: Today, I am grateful for...

1.

2.

3.

Intention: Today, my intention is...

Committed Action: Today, the actions I will take to manifest my goals, dreams, and intentions are...

Date:

Gratitudes: Today, I am grateful for...

1.

2.

3.

Intention: Today, my intention is...

Committed Action: Today, the actions I will take to manifest my goals, dreams, and intentions are...

Date:

Gratitudes: Today, I am grateful for...

1.

2.

3.

Intention: Today, my intention is...

Committed Action: Today, the actions I will take to manifest my goals, dreams, and intentions are...

Date:

Gratitudes: Today, I am grateful for...

1.

2.

3.

Intention: Today, my intention is...

Committed Action: Today, the actions I will take to manifest my goals, dreams, and intentions are...

Date:

Gratitudes: Today, I am grateful for...

1.

2.

3.

Intention: Today, my intention is...

Committed Action: Today, the actions I will take to manifest my goals, dreams, and intentions are...

Date:

Gratitudes: Today, I am grateful for...

1.

2.

3.

Intention: Today, my intention is...

Committed Action: Today, the actions I will take to manifest my goals, dreams, and intentions are...

Date:

Gratitudes: Today, I am grateful for...

1.

2.

3.

Intention: Today, my intention is...

Committed Action: Today, the actions I will take to manifest my goals, dreams, and intentions are...

Date:

Gratitudes: Today, I am grateful for...

1.

2.

3.

Intention: Today, my intention is...

Committed Action: Today, the actions I will take to manifest my goals, dreams, and intentions are...

Date:

Gratitudes: Today, I am grateful for...

1.

2.

3.

Intention: Today, my intention is...

Committed Action: Today, the actions I will take to manifest my goals, dreams, and intentions are...

Date:

Gratitudes: Today, I am grateful for...

1.

2.

3.

Intention: Today, my intention is...

Committed Action: Today, the actions I will take to manifest my goals, dreams, and intentions are...

Date:

Gratitudes: Today, I am grateful for...

1.

2.

3.

Intention: Today, my intention is...

Committed Action: Today, the actions I will take to manifest my goals, dreams, and intentions are...

Date:

Gratitudes: Today, I am grateful for...

1.

2.

3.

Intention: Today, my intention is...

Committed Action: Today, the actions I will take to manifest my goals, dreams, and intentions are...

Date:

Gratitudes: Today, I am grateful for...

1.

2.

3.

Intention: Today, my intention is...

Committed Action: Today, the actions I will take to manifest my goals, dreams, and intentions are...

Date:

Gratitudes: Today, I am grateful for...

1.

2.

3.

Intention: Today, my intention is...

Committed Action: Today, the actions I will take to manifest my goals, dreams, and intentions are...

Date:

Gratitudes: Today, I am grateful for...

1.

2.

3.

Intention: Today, my intention is...

Committed Action: Today, the actions I will take to manifest my goals, dreams, and intentions are...

Date:

Gratitudes: Today, I am grateful for...

1.

2.

3.

Intention: Today, my intention is...

Committed Action: Today, the actions I will take to manifest my goals, dreams, and intentions are...

Date:

Gratitudes: Today, I am grateful for...

1.

2.

3.

Intention: Today, my intention is...

Committed Action: Today, the actions I will take to manifest my goals, dreams, and intentions are...

Date:

Gratitudes: Today, I am grateful for...

1.

2.

3.

Intention: Today, my intention is...

Committed Action: Today, the actions I will take to manifest my goals, dreams, and intentions are...

Date:

Gratitudes: Today, I am grateful for...

1.

2.

3.

Intention: Today, my intention is...

Committed Action: Today, the actions I will take to manifest my goals, dreams, and intentions are...

Date:

Gratitudes: Today, I am grateful for...

1.

2.

3.

Intention: Today, my intention is...

Committed Action: Today, the actions I will take to manifest my goals, dreams, and intentions are...

Date:

Gratitudes: Today, I am grateful for...

1.

2.

3.

Intention: Today, my intention is...

Committed Action: Today, the actions I will take to manifest my goals, dreams, and intentions are...

Date:

Gratitudes: Today, I am grateful for...

1.

2.

3.

Intention: Today, my intention is...

Committed Action: Today, the actions I will take to manifest my goals, dreams, and intentions are...

Date:

Gratitudes: Today, I am grateful for...

1.

2.

3.

Intention: Today, my intention is...

Committed Action: Today, the actions I will take to manifest my goals, dreams, and intentions are...

Date:

Gratitudes: Today, I am grateful for...

1.

2.

3.

Intention: Today, my intention is...

Committed Action: Today, the actions I will take to manifest my goals, dreams, and intentions are...

Date:

Gratitudes: Today, I am grateful for...

1.

2.

3.

Intention: Today, my intention is...

Committed Action: Today, the actions I will take to manifest my goals, dreams, and intentions are...

Date:

Gratitudes: Today, I am grateful for...

1.

2.

3.

Intention: Today, my intention is...

Committed Action: Today, the actions I will take to manifest my goals, dreams, and intentions are...

Date:

Gratitudes: Today, I am grateful for...

1.

2.

3.

Intention: Today, my intention is...

Committed Action: Today, the actions I will take to manifest my goals, dreams, and intentions are...

Date:

Gratitudes: Today, I am grateful for...

1.

2.

3.

Intention: Today, my intention is...

Committed Action: Today, the actions I will take to manifest my goals, dreams, and intentions are...

Date:

Gratitudes: Today, I am grateful for...

1.

2.

3.

Intention: Today, my intention is...

Committed Action: Today, the actions I will take to manifest my goals, dreams, and intentions are...

Date:

Gratitudes: Today, I am grateful for...

1.

2.

3.

Intention: Today, my intention is...

Committed Action: Today, the actions I will take to manifest my goals, dreams, and intentions are...

Date:

Gratitudes: Today, I am grateful for...

1.

2.

3.

Intention: Today, my intention is...

Committed Action: Today, the actions I will take to manifest my goals, dreams, and intentions are...

Date:

Gratitudes: Today, I am grateful for...

1.

2.

3.

Intention: Today, my intention is...

Committed Action: Today, the actions I will take to manifest my goals, dreams, and intentions are...

Date:

Gratitudes: Today, I am grateful for...

1.

2.

3.

Intention: Today, my intention is...

Committed Action: Today, the actions I will take to manifest my goals, dreams, and intentions are...

Date:

Gratitudes: Today, I am grateful for...

1.

2.

3.

Intention: Today, my intention is...

Committed Action: Today, the actions I will take to manifest my goals, dreams, and intentions are...

Date:

Gratitudes: Today, I am grateful for...

1.

2.

3.

Intention: Today, my intention is...

Committed Action: Today, the actions I will take to manifest my goals, dreams, and intentions are...

Date:

Gratitudes: Today, I am grateful for...

1.

2.

3.

Intention: Today, my intention is...

Committed Action: Today, the actions I will take to manifest my goals, dreams, and intentions are...

Date:

Gratitudes: Today, I am grateful for...

1.

2.

3.

Intention: Today, my intention is...

Committed Action: Today, the actions I will take to manifest my goals, dreams, and intentions are...

Date:

Gratitudes: Today, I am grateful for...

1.

2.

3.

Intention: Today, my intention is...

Committed Action: Today, the actions I will take to manifest my goals, dreams, and intentions are...

Date:

Gratitudes: Today, I am grateful for...

1.

2.

3.

Intention: Today, my intention is...

Committed Action: Today, the actions I will take to manifest my goals, dreams, and intentions are...

Date:

Gratitudes: Today, I am grateful for...

1.

2.

3.

Intention: Today, my intention is...

Committed Action: Today, the actions I will take to manifest my goals, dreams, and intentions are...

Date:

Gratitudes: Today, I am grateful for...

1.

2.

3.

Intention: Today, my intention is...

Committed Action: Today, the actions I will take to manifest my goals, dreams, and intentions are...

Date:

Gratitudes: Today, I am grateful for...

1.

2.

3.

Intention: Today, my intention is...

Committed Action: Today, the actions I will take to manifest my goals, dreams, and intentions are...

Date:

Gratitudes: Today, I am grateful for...

1.

2.

3.

Intention: Today, my intention is...

Committed Action: Today, the actions I will take to manifest my goals, dreams, and intentions are...

Date:

Gratitudes: Today, I am grateful for...

1.

2.

3.

Intention: Today, my intention is...

Committed Action: Today, the actions I will take to manifest my goals, dreams, and intentions are...

Date:

Gratitudes: Today, I am grateful for...

1.

2.

3.

Intention: Today, my intention is...

Committed Action: Today, the actions I will take to manifest my goals, dreams, and intentions are...

Date:

Gratitudes: Today, I am grateful for...

1.

2.

3.

Intention: Today, my intention is...

Committed Action: Today, the actions I will take to manifest my goals, dreams, and intentions are...

Date:

Gratitudes: Today, I am grateful for...

1.

2.

3.

Intention: Today, my intention is...

Committed Action: Today, the actions I will take to manifest my goals, dreams, and intentions are...

Date:

Gratitudes: Today, I am grateful for...

1.

2.

3.

Intention: Today, my intention is...

Committed Action: Today, the actions I will take to manifest my goals, dreams, and intentions are...

Date:

Gratitudes: Today, I am grateful for...

1.

2.

3.

Intention: Today, my intention is...

Committed Action: Today, the actions I will take to manifest my goals, dreams, and intentions are...

Date:

Gratitudes: Today, I am grateful for...

1.

2.

3.

Intention: Today, my intention is...

Committed Action: Today, the actions I will take to manifest my goals, dreams, and intentions are...

Date:

Gratitudes: Today, I am grateful for...

1.

2.

3.

Intention: Today, my intention is...

Committed Action: Today, the actions I will take to manifest my goals, dreams, and intentions are...

Date:

Gratitudes: Today, I am grateful for...

1.

2.

3.

Intention: Today, my intention is...

Committed Action: Today, the actions I will take to manifest my goals, dreams, and intentions are...

Date:

Gratitudes: Today, I am grateful for...

1.

2.

3.

Intention: Today, my intention is...

Committed Action: Today, the actions I will take to manifest my goals, dreams, and intentions are...

Date:

Gratitudes: Today, I am grateful for...

1.

2.

3.

Intention: Today, my intention is...

Committed Action: Today, the actions I will take to manifest my goals, dreams, and intentions are...

Date:

Gratitudes: Today, I am grateful for...

1.

2.

3.

Intention: Today, my intention is...

Committed Action: Today, the actions I will take to manifest my goals, dreams, and intentions are...

Date:

Gratitudes: Today, I am grateful for...

1.

2.

3.

Intention: Today, my intention is...

Committed Action: Today, the actions I will take to manifest my goals, dreams, and intentions are...

Date:

Gratitudes: Today, I am grateful for...

1.

2.

3.

Intention: Today, my intention is...

Committed Action: Today, the actions I will take to manifest my goals, dreams, and intentions are...

Date:

Gratitudes: Today, I am grateful for...

1.

2.

3.

Intention: Today, my intention is...

Committed Action: Today, the actions I will take to manifest my goals, dreams, and intentions are...

Date:

Gratitudes: Today, I am grateful for...

1.

2.

3.

Intention: Today, my intention is...

Committed Action: Today, the actions I will take to manifest my goals, dreams, and intentions are...

Date:

Gratitudes: Today, I am grateful for...

1.

2.

3.

Intention: Today, my intention is...

Committed Action: Today, the actions I will take to manifest my goals, dreams, and intentions are...

Date:

Gratitudes: Today, I am grateful for...

1.

2.

3.

Intention: Today, my intention is...

Committed Action: Today, the actions I will take to manifest my goals, dreams, and intentions are...

Date:

Gratitudes: Today, I am grateful for...

1.

2.

3.

Intention: Today, my intention is...

Committed Action: Today, the actions I will take to manifest my goals, dreams, and intentions are...

Date:

Gratitudes: Today, I am grateful for...

1.

2.

3.

Intention: Today, my intention is...

Committed Action: Today, the actions I will take to manifest my goals, dreams, and intentions are...

Date:

Gratitudes: Today, I am grateful for...

1.

2.

3.

Intention: Today, my intention is...

Committed Action: Today, the actions I will take to manifest my goals, dreams, and intentions are...

Date:

Gratitudes: Today, I am grateful for...

1.

2.

3.

Intention: Today, my intention is...

Committed Action: Today, the actions I will take to manifest my goals, dreams, and intentions are...

Date:

Gratitudes: Today, I am grateful for...

1.

2.

3.

Intention: Today, my intention is...

Committed Action: Today, the actions I will take to manifest my goals, dreams, and intentions are...

Date:

Gratitudes: Today, I am grateful for...

1.

2.

3.

Intention: Today, my intention is...

Committed Action: Today, the actions I will take to manifest my goals, dreams, and intentions are...

Date:

Gratitudes: Today, I am grateful for...

1.

2.

3.

Intention: Today, my intention is...

Committed Action: Today, the actions I will take to manifest my goals, dreams, and intentions are...

Date:

Gratitudes: Today, I am grateful for...

1.

2.

3.

Intention: Today, my intention is...

Committed Action: Today, the actions I will take to manifest my goals, dreams, and intentions are...

Date:

Gratitudes: Today, I am grateful for...

1.

2.

3.

Intention: Today, my intention is...

Committed Action: Today, the actions I will take to manifest my goals, dreams, and intentions are...

Date:

Gratitudes: Today, I am grateful for...

1.

2.

3.

Intention: Today, my intention is...

Committed Action: Today, the actions I will take to manifest my goals, dreams, and intentions are...

Date:

Gratitudes: Today, I am grateful for...

1.

2.

3.

Intention: Today, my intention is...

Committed Action: Today, the actions I will take to manifest my goals, dreams, and intentions are...

Date:

Gratitudes: Today, I am grateful for...

1.

2.

3.

Intention: Today, my intention is...

Committed Action: Today, the actions I will take to manifest my goals, dreams, and intentions are...

Date:

Gratitudes: Today, I am grateful for...

1.

2.

3.

Intention: Today, my intention is...

Committed Action: Today, the actions I will take to manifest my goals, dreams, and intentions are...

Date:

Gratitudes: Today, I am grateful for...

1.

2.

3.

Intention: Today, my intention is...

Committed Action: Today, the actions I will take to manifest my goals, dreams, and intentions are...

Date:

Gratitudes: Today, I am grateful for...

1.

2.

3.

Intention: Today, my intention is...

Committed Action: Today, the actions I will take to manifest my goals, dreams, and intentions are...

Date:

Gratitudes: Today, I am grateful for...

1.

2.

3.

Intention: Today, my intention is...

Committed Action: Today, the actions I will take to manifest my goals, dreams, and intentions are...

Date:

Gratitudes: Today, I am grateful for...

1.

2.

3.

Intention: Today, my intention is...

Committed Action: Today, the actions I will take to manifest my goals, dreams, and intentions are...

Date:

Gratitudes: Today, I am grateful for...

1.

2.

3.

Intention: Today, my intention is...

Committed Action: Today, the actions I will take to manifest my goals, dreams, and intentions are...

Date:

Gratitudes: Today, I am grateful for...

1.

2.

3.

Intention: Today, my intention is...

Committed Action: Today, the actions I will take to manifest my goals, dreams, and intentions are...

Date:

Gratitudes: Today, I am grateful for...

1.

2.

3.

Intention: Today, my intention is...

Committed Action: Today, the actions I will take to manifest my goals, dreams, and intentions are...

Date:

Gratitudes: Today, I am grateful for...

1.

2.

3.

Intention: Today, my intention is...

Committed Action: Today, the actions I will take to manifest my goals, dreams, and intentions are...

Date:

Gratitudes: Today, I am grateful for...

1.

2.

3.

Intention: Today, my intention is...

Committed Action: Today, the actions I will take to manifest my goals, dreams, and intentions are...

Date:

Gratitudes: Today, I am grateful for...

1.

2.

3.

Intention: Today, my intention is...

Committed Action: Today, the actions I will take to manifest my goals, dreams, and intentions are...

Date:

Gratitudes: Today, I am grateful for...

1.

2.

3.

Intention: Today, my intention is...

Committed Action: Today, the actions I will take to manifest my goals, dreams, and intentions are...

Date:

Gratitudes: Today, I am grateful for...

1.

2.

3.

Intention: Today, my intention is...

Committed Action: Today, the actions I will take to manifest my goals, dreams, and intentions are...

Date:

Gratitudes: Today, I am grateful for...

1.

2.

3.

Intention: Today, my intention is...

Committed Action: Today, the actions I will take to manifest my goals, dreams, and intentions are...

Date:

Gratitudes: Today, I am grateful for...

1.

2.

3.

Intention: Today, my intention is...

Committed Action: Today, the actions I will take to manifest my goals, dreams, and intentions are...

Date:

Gratitudes: Today, I am grateful for...

1.

2.

3.

Intention: Today, my intention is...

Committed Action: Today, the actions I will take to manifest my goals, dreams, and intentions are...

Date:

Gratitudes: Today, I am grateful for...

1.

2.

3.

Intention: Today, my intention is...

Committed Action: Today, the actions I will take to manifest my goals, dreams, and intentions are...

Date:

Gratitudes: Today, I am grateful for...

1.

2.

3.

Intention: Today, my intention is...

Committed Action: Today, the actions I will take to manifest my goals, dreams, and intentions are...

Date:

Gratitudes: Today, I am grateful for...

1.

2.

3.

Intention: Today, my intention is...

Committed Action: Today, the actions I will take to manifest my goals, dreams, and intentions are...

Date:

Gratitudes: Today, I am grateful for...

1.

2.

3.

Intention: Today, my intention is...

Committed Action: Today, the actions I will take to manifest my goals, dreams, and intentions are...

Date:

Gratitudes: Today, I am grateful for...

1.

2.

3.

Intention: Today, my intention is...

Committed Action: Today, the actions I will take to manifest my goals, dreams, and intentions are...

Date:

Gratitudes: Today, I am grateful for...

1.

2.

3.

Intention: Today, my intention is...

Committed Action: Today, the actions I will take to manifest my goals, dreams, and intentions are...

Date:

Gratitudes: Today, I am grateful for...

1.

2.

3.

Intention: Today, my intention is...

Committed Action: Today, the actions I will take to manifest my goals, dreams, and intentions are...

Date:

Gratitudes: Today, I am grateful for...

1.

2.

3.

Intention: Today, my intention is...

Committed Action: Today, the actions I will take to manifest my goals, dreams, and intentions are...

Date:

Gratitudes: Today, I am grateful for...

1.

2.

3.

Intention: Today, my intention is...

Committed Action: Today, the actions I will take to manifest my goals, dreams, and intentions are...

Date:

Gratitudes: Today, I am grateful for…

1.

2.

3.

Intention: Today, my intention is…

Committed Action: Today, the actions I will take to manifest my goals, dreams, and intentions are…

Date:

Gratitudes: Today, I am grateful for...

1.

2.

3.

Intention: Today, my intention is...

Committed Action: Today, the actions I will take to manifest my goals, dreams, and intentions are...

Date:

Gratitudes: Today, I am grateful for...

1.

2.

3.

Intention: Today, my intention is...

Committed Action: Today, the actions I will take to manifest my goals, dreams, and intentions are...

Date:

Gratitudes: Today, I am grateful for...

1.

2.

3.

Intention: Today, my intention is...

Committed Action: Today, the actions I will take to manifest my goals, dreams, and intentions are...

Date:

Gratitudes: Today, I am grateful for...

1.

2.

3.

Intention: Today, my intention is...

Committed Action: Today, the actions I will take to manifest my goals, dreams, and intentions are...

Date:

Gratitudes: Today, I am grateful for...

1.

2.

3.

Intention: Today, my intention is...

Committed Action: Today, the actions I will take to manifest my goals, dreams, and intentions are...

Date:

Gratitudes: Today, I am grateful for...

1.

2.

3.

Intention: Today, my intention is...

Committed Action: Today, the actions I will take to manifest my goals, dreams, and intentions are...

Date:

Gratitudes: Today, I am grateful for...

1.

2.

3.

Intention: Today, my intention is...

Committed Action: Today, the actions I will take to manifest my goals, dreams, and intentions are...

Date:

Gratitudes: Today, I am grateful for...

1.

2.

3.

Intention: Today, my intention is...

Committed Action: Today, the actions I will take to manifest my goals, dreams, and intentions are...

Date:

Gratitudes: Today, I am grateful for...

1.

2.

3.

Intention: Today, my intention is...

Committed Action: Today, the actions I will take to manifest my goals, dreams, and intentions are...

Date:

Gratitudes: Today, I am grateful for...

1.

2.

3.

Intention: Today, my intention is...

Committed Action: Today, the actions I will take to manifest my goals, dreams, and intentions are...

Date:

Gratitudes: Today, I am grateful for...

1.

2.

3.

Intention: Today, my intention is...

Committed Action: Today, the actions I will take to manifest my goals, dreams, and intentions are...

Date:

Gratitudes: Today, I am grateful for...

1.

2.

3.

Intention: Today, my intention is...

Committed Action: Today, the actions I will take to manifest my goals, dreams, and intentions are...

Date:

Gratitudes: Today, I am grateful for...

1.

2.

3.

Intention: Today, my intention is...

Committed Action: Today, the actions I will take to manifest my goals, dreams, and intentions are...

Date:

Gratitudes: Today, I am grateful for...

1.

2.

3.

Intention: Today, my intention is...

Committed Action: Today, the actions I will take to manifest my goals, dreams, and intentions are...

Date:

Gratitudes: Today, I am grateful for...

1.

2.

3.

Intention: Today, my intention is...

Committed Action: Today, the actions I will take to manifest my goals, dreams, and intentions are...

Date:

Gratitudes: Today, I am grateful for...

1.

2.

3.

Intention: Today, my intention is...

Committed Action: Today, the actions I will take to manifest my goals, dreams, and intentions are...

Date:

Gratitudes: Today, I am grateful for...

1.

2.

3.

Intention: Today, my intention is...

Committed Action: Today, the actions I will take to manifest my goals, dreams, and intentions are...

Date:

Gratitudes: Today, I am grateful for...

1.

2.

3.

Intention: Today, my intention is...

Committed Action: Today, the actions I will take to manifest my goals, dreams, and intentions are...

Date:

Gratitudes: Today, I am grateful for...

1.

2.

3.

Intention: Today, my intention is...

Committed Action: Today, the actions I will take to manifest my goals, dreams, and intentions are...

Date:

Gratitudes: Today, I am grateful for...

1.

2.

3.

Intention: Today, my intention is...

Committed Action: Today, the actions I will take to manifest my goals, dreams, and intentions are...

Date:

Gratitudes: Today, I am grateful for...

1.

2.

3.

Intention: Today, my intention is...

Committed Action: Today, the actions I will take to manifest my goals, dreams, and intentions are...

Date:

Gratitudes: Today, I am grateful for...

1.

2.

3.

Intention: Today, my intention is...

Committed Action: Today, the actions I will take to manifest my goals, dreams, and intentions are...

Date:

Gratitudes: Today, I am grateful for...

1.

2.

3.

Intention: Today, my intention is...

Committed Action: Today, the actions I will take to manifest my goals, dreams, and intentions are...

Date:

Gratitudes: Today, I am grateful for...

1.

2.

3.

Intention: Today, my intention is...

Committed Action: Today, the actions I will take to manifest my goals, dreams, and intentions are...

Date:

Gratitudes: Today, I am grateful for...

1.

2.

3.

Intention: Today, my intention is...

Committed Action: Today, the actions I will take to manifest my goals, dreams, and intentions are...

Date:

Gratitudes: Today, I am grateful for...

1.

2.

3.

Intention: Today, my intention is...

Committed Action: Today, the actions I will take to manifest my goals, dreams, and intentions are...

Date:

Gratitudes: Today, I am grateful for...

1.

2.

3.

Intention: Today, my intention is...

Committed Action: Today, the actions I will take to manifest my goals, dreams, and intentions are...

Date:

Gratitudes: Today, I am grateful for...

1.

2.

3.

Intention: Today, my intention is...

Committed Action: Today, the actions I will take to manifest my goals, dreams, and intentions are...

Date:

Gratitudes: Today, I am grateful for...

1.

2.

3.

Intention: Today, my intention is...

Committed Action: Today, the actions I will take to manifest my goals, dreams, and intentions are...

Date:

Gratitudes: Today, I am grateful for...

1.

2.

3.

Intention: Today, my intention is...

Committed Action: Today, the actions I will take to manifest my goals, dreams, and intentions are...

Date:

Gratitudes: Today, I am grateful for...

1.

2.

3.

Intention: Today, my intention is...

Committed Action: Today, the actions I will take to manifest my goals, dreams, and intentions are...

Date:

Gratitudes: Today, I am grateful for...

1.

2.

3.

Intention: Today, my intention is...

Committed Action: Today, the actions I will take to manifest my goals, dreams, and intentions are...

Date:

Gratitudes: Today, I am grateful for...

1.

2.

3.

Intention: Today, my intention is...

Committed Action: Today, the actions I will take to manifest my goals, dreams, and intentions are...

Date:

Gratitudes: Today, I am grateful for...

1.

2.

3.

Intention: Today, my intention is...

Committed Action: Today, the actions I will take to manifest my goals, dreams, and intentions are...

Date:

Gratitudes: Today, I am grateful for...

1.

2.

3.

Intention: Today, my intention is...

Committed Action: Today, the actions I will take to manifest my goals, dreams, and intentions are...

Date:

Gratitudes: Today, I am grateful for...

1.

2.

3.

Intention: Today, my intention is...

Committed Action: Today, the actions I will take to manifest my goals, dreams, and intentions are...

Date:

Gratitudes: Today, I am grateful for...

1.

2.

3.

Intention: Today, my intention is...

Committed Action: Today, the actions I will take to manifest my goals, dreams, and intentions are...

Date:

Gratitudes: Today, I am grateful for...

1.

2.

3.

Intention: Today, my intention is...

Committed Action: Today, the actions I will take to manifest my goals, dreams, and intentions are...

Date:

Gratitudes: Today, I am grateful for...

1.

2.

3.

Intention: Today, my intention is...

Committed Action: Today, the actions I will take to manifest my goals, dreams, and intentions are...

Date:

Gratitudes: Today, I am grateful for...

1.

2.

3.

Intention: Today, my intention is...

Committed Action: Today, the actions I will take to manifest my goals, dreams, and intentions are...

Date:

Gratitudes: Today, I am grateful for...

1.

2.

3.

Intention: Today, my intention is...

Committed Action: Today, the actions I will take to manifest my goals, dreams, and intentions are...

Date:

Gratitudes: Today, I am grateful for...

1.

2.

3.

Intention: Today, my intention is...

Committed Action: Today, the actions I will take to manifest my goals, dreams, and intentions are...

Date:

Gratitudes: Today, I am grateful for...

1.

2.

3.

Intention: Today, my intention is...

Committed Action: Today, the actions I will take to manifest my goals, dreams, and intentions are...

Date:

Gratitudes: Today, I am grateful for...

1.

2.

3.

Intention: Today, my intention is...

Committed Action: Today, the actions I will take to manifest my goals, dreams, and intentions are...

Date:

Gratitudes: Today, I am grateful for...

1.

2.

3.

Intention: Today, my intention is...

Committed Action: Today, the actions I will take to manifest my goals, dreams, and intentions are...

Date:

Gratitudes: Today, I am grateful for...

1.

2.

3.

Intention: Today, my intention is...

Committed Action: Today, the actions I will take to manifest my goals, dreams, and intentions are...

Date:

Gratitudes: Today, I am grateful for...

1.

2.

3.

Intention: Today, my intention is...

Committed Action: Today, the actions I will take to manifest my goals, dreams, and intentions are...

Date:

Gratitudes: Today, I am grateful for...

1.

2.

3.

Intention: Today, my intention is...

Committed Action: Today, the actions I will take to manifest my goals, dreams, and intentions are...

Date:

Gratitudes: Today, I am grateful for...

1.

2.

3.

Intention: Today, my intention is...

Committed Action: Today, the actions I will take to manifest my goals, dreams, and intentions are...

Date:

Gratitudes: Today, I am grateful for...

1.

2.

3.

Intention: Today, my intention is...

Committed Action: Today, the actions I will take to manifest my goals, dreams, and intentions are...

Date:

Gratitudes: Today, I am grateful for…

1.

2.

3.

Intention: Today, my intention is…

Committed Action: Today, the actions I will take to manifest my goals,
dreams, and intentions are…

Date:

Gratitudes: Today, I am grateful for...

1.

2.

3.

Intention: Today, my intention is...

Committed Action: Today, the actions I will take to manifest my goals, dreams, and intentions are...

Date:

Gratitudes: Today, I am grateful for...

1.

2.

3.

Intention: Today, my intention is...

Committed Action: Today, the actions I will take to manifest my goals, dreams, and intentions are...

Date:

Gratitudes: Today, I am grateful for...

1.

2.

3.

Intention: Today, my intention is...

Committed Action: Today, the actions I will take to manifest my goals, dreams, and intentions are...

Date:

Gratitudes: Today, I am grateful for...

1.

2.

3.

Intention: Today, my intention is...

Committed Action: Today, the actions I will take to manifest my goals, dreams, and intentions are...

Date:

Gratitudes: Today, I am grateful for...

1.

2.

3.

Intention: Today, my intention is...

Committed Action: Today, the actions I will take to manifest my goals, dreams, and intentions are...

Date:

Gratitudes: Today, I am grateful for...

1.

2.

3.

Intention: Today, my intention is...

Committed Action: Today, the actions I will take to manifest my goals, dreams, and intentions are...

Date:

Gratitudes: Today, I am grateful for...

1.

2.

3.

Intention: Today, my intention is...

Committed Action: Today, the actions I will take to manifest my goals, dreams, and intentions are...

Date:

Gratitudes: Today, I am grateful for...

1.

2.

3.

Intention: Today, my intention is...

Committed Action: Today, the actions I will take to manifest my goals, dreams, and intentions are...

Date:

Gratitudes: Today, I am grateful for…

1.

2.

3.

Intention: Today, my intention is…

Committed Action: Today, the actions I will take to manifest my goals, dreams, and intentions are…

Date:

Gratitudes: Today, I am grateful for...

1.

2.

3.

Intention: Today, my intention is...

Committed Action: Today, the actions I will take to manifest my goals, dreams, and intentions are...

Date:

Gratitudes: Today, I am grateful for...

1.

2.

3.

Intention: Today, my intention is...

Committed Action: Today, the actions I will take to manifest my goals, dreams, and intentions are...

Date:

Gratitudes: Today, I am grateful for...

1.

2.

3.

Intention: Today, my intention is...

Committed Action: Today, the actions I will take to manifest my goals, dreams, and intentions are...

Date:

Gratitudes: Today, I am grateful for...

1.

2.

3.

Intention: Today, my intention is...

Committed Action: Today, the actions I will take to manifest my goals, dreams, and intentions are...

Date:

Gratitudes: Today, I am grateful for...

1.

2.

3.

Intention: Today, my intention is...

Committed Action: Today, the actions I will take to manifest my goals, dreams, and intentions are...

Date:

Gratitudes: Today, I am grateful for...

1.

2.

3.

Intention: Today, my intention is...

Committed Action: Today, the actions I will take to manifest my goals, dreams, and intentions are...

Date:

Gratitudes: Today, I am grateful for...

1.

2.

3.

Intention: Today, my intention is...

Committed Action: Today, the actions I will take to manifest my goals, dreams, and intentions are...

Date:

Gratitudes: Today, I am grateful for...

1.

2.

3.

Intention: Today, my intention is...

Committed Action: Today, the actions I will take to manifest my goals, dreams, and intentions are...

Date:

Gratitudes: Today, I am grateful for...

1.

2.

3.

Intention: Today, my intention is...

Committed Action: Today, the actions I will take to manifest my goals, dreams, and intentions are...

Date:

Gratitudes: Today, I am grateful for...

1.

2.

3.

Intention: Today, my intention is...

Committed Action: Today, the actions I will take to manifest my goals, dreams, and intentions are...

Date:

Gratitudes: Today, I am grateful for...

1.

2.

3.

Intention: Today, my intention is...

Committed Action: Today, the actions I will take to manifest my goals, dreams, and intentions are...

Date:

Gratitudes: Today, I am grateful for...

1.

2.

3.

Intention: Today, my intention is...

Committed Action: Today, the actions I will take to manifest my goals, dreams, and intentions are...

Date:

Gratitudes: Today, I am grateful for...

1.

2.

3.

Intention: Today, my intention is...

Committed Action: Today, the actions I will take to manifest my goals, dreams, and intentions are...

Date:

Gratitudes: Today, I am grateful for...

1.

2.

3.

Intention: Today, my intention is...

Committed Action: Today, the actions I will take to manifest my goals, dreams, and intentions are...

Date:

Gratitudes: Today, I am grateful for...

1.

2.

3.

Intention: Today, my intention is...

Committed Action: Today, the actions I will take to manifest my goals, dreams, and intentions are...

Date:

Gratitudes: Today, I am grateful for...

1.

2.

3.

Intention: Today, my intention is...

Committed Action: Today, the actions I will take to manifest my goals, dreams, and intentions are...

Date:

Gratitudes: Today, I am grateful for...

1.

2.

3.

Intention: Today, my intention is...

Committed Action: Today, the actions I will take to manifest my goals, dreams, and intentions are...

Date:

Gratitudes: Today, I am grateful for...

1.

2.

3.

Intention: Today, my intention is...

Committed Action: Today, the actions I will take to manifest my goals, dreams, and intentions are...

Date:

Gratitudes: Today, I am grateful for...

1.

2.

3.

Intention: Today, my intention is...

Committed Action: Today, the actions I will take to manifest my goals, dreams, and intentions are...

Date:

Gratitudes: Today, I am grateful for...

1.

2.

3.

Intention: Today, my intention is...

Committed Action: Today, the actions I will take to manifest my goals, dreams, and intentions are...

Date:

Gratitudes: Today, I am grateful for...

1.

2.

3.

Intention: Today, my intention is...

Committed Action: Today, the actions I will take to manifest my goals, dreams, and intentions are...

Date:

Gratitudes: Today, I am grateful for...

1.

2.

3.

Intention: Today, my intention is...

Committed Action: Today, the actions I will take to manifest my goals, dreams, and intentions are...

Date:

Gratitudes: Today, I am grateful for...

1.

2.

3.

Intention: Today, my intention is...

Committed Action: Today, the actions I will take to manifest my goals, dreams, and intentions are...

Date:

Gratitudes: Today, I am grateful for...

1.

2.

3.

Intention: Today, my intention is...

Committed Action: Today, the actions I will take to manifest my goals, dreams, and intentions are...

Date:

Gratitudes: Today, I am grateful for...

1.

2.

3.

Intention: Today, my intention is...

Committed Action: Today, the actions I will take to manifest my goals, dreams, and intentions are...

Date:

Gratitudes: Today, I am grateful for...

1.

2.

3.

Intention: Today, my intention is...

Committed Action: Today, the actions I will take to manifest my goals, dreams, and intentions are...

Date:

Gratitudes: Today, I am grateful for...

1.

2.

3.

Intention: Today, my intention is...

Committed Action: Today, the actions I will take to manifest my goals, dreams, and intentions are...

Date:

Gratitudes: Today, I am grateful for...

1.

2.

3.

Intention: Today, my intention is...

Committed Action: Today, the actions I will take to manifest my goals, dreams, and intentions are...

Date:

Gratitudes: Today, I am grateful for...

1.

2.

3.

Intention: Today, my intention is...

Committed Action: Today, the actions I will take to manifest my goals, dreams, and intentions are...

Date:

Gratitudes: Today, I am grateful for...

1.

2.

3.

Intention: Today, my intention is...

Committed Action: Today, the actions I will take to manifest my goals, dreams, and intentions are...

Date:

Gratitudes: Today, I am grateful for...

1.

2.

3.

Intention: Today, my intention is...

Committed Action: Today, the actions I will take to manifest my goals, dreams, and intentions are...

Date:

Gratitudes: Today, I am grateful for...

1.

2.

3.

Intention: Today, my intention is...

Committed Action: Today, the actions I will take to manifest my goals, dreams, and intentions are...

Date:

Gratitudes: Today, I am grateful for...

1.

2.

3.

Intention: Today, my intention is...

Committed Action: Today, the actions I will take to manifest my goals, dreams, and intentions are...

Date:

Gratitudes: Today, I am grateful for...

1.

2.

3.

Intention: Today, my intention is...

Committed Action: Today, the actions I will take to manifest my goals, dreams, and intentions are...

Date:

Gratitudes: Today, I am grateful for...

1.

2.

3.

Intention: Today, my intention is...

Committed Action: Today, the actions I will take to manifest my goals, dreams, and intentions are...

Date:

Gratitudes: Today, I am grateful for...

1.

2.

3.

Intention: Today, my intention is...

Committed Action: Today, the actions I will take to manifest my goals, dreams, and intentions are...

Date:

Gratitudes: Today, I am grateful for...

1.

2.

3.

Intention: Today, my intention is...

Committed Action: Today, the actions I will take to manifest my goals, dreams, and intentions are...

Date:

Gratitudes: Today, I am grateful for...

1.

2.

3.

Intention: Today, my intention is...

Committed Action: Today, the actions I will take to manifest my goals, dreams, and intentions are...

Date:

Gratitudes: Today, I am grateful for...

1.

2.

3.

Intention: Today, my intention is...

Committed Action: Today, the actions I will take to manifest my goals, dreams, and intentions are...

Date:

Gratitudes: Today, I am grateful for...

1.

2.

3.

Intention: Today, my intention is...

Committed Action: Today, the actions I will take to manifest my goals, dreams, and intentions are...

Date:

Gratitudes: Today, I am grateful for...

1.

2.

3.

Intention: Today, my intention is...

Committed Action: Today, the actions I will take to manifest my goals, dreams, and intentions are...

Date:

Gratitudes: Today, I am grateful for...

1.

2.

3.

Intention: Today, my intention is...

Committed Action: Today, the actions I will take to manifest my goals, dreams, and intentions are...

Date:

Gratitudes: Today, I am grateful for...

1.

2.

3.

Intention: Today, my intention is...

Committed Action: Today, the actions I will take to manifest my goals, dreams, and intentions are...

Date:

Gratitudes: Today, I am grateful for...

1.

2.

3.

Intention: Today, my intention is...

Committed Action: Today, the actions I will take to manifest my goals, dreams, and intentions are...

Date:

Gratitudes: Today, I am grateful for...

1.

2.

3.

Intention: Today, my intention is...

Committed Action: Today, the actions I will take to manifest my goals, dreams, and intentions are...

Date:

Gratitudes: Today, I am grateful for...

1.

2.

3.

Intention: Today, my intention is...

Committed Action: Today, the actions I will take to manifest my goals, dreams, and intentions are...

Date:

Gratitudes: Today, I am grateful for...

1.

2.

3.

Intention: Today, my intention is...

Committed Action: Today, the actions I will take to manifest my goals, dreams, and intentions are...

Date:

Gratitudes: Today, I am grateful for...

1.

2.

3.

Intention: Today, my intention is...

Committed Action: Today, the actions I will take to manifest my goals, dreams, and intentions are...

Date:

Gratitudes: Today, I am grateful for...

1.

2.

3.

Intention: Today, my intention is...

Committed Action: Today, the actions I will take to manifest my goals, dreams, and intentions are...

Date:

Gratitudes: Today, I am grateful for...

1.

2.

3.

Intention: Today, my intention is...

Committed Action: Today, the actions I will take to manifest my goals, dreams, and intentions are...

Date:

Gratitudes: Today, I am grateful for...

1.

2.

3.

Intention: Today, my intention is...

Committed Action: Today, the actions I will take to manifest my goals, dreams, and intentions are...

Date:

Gratitudes: Today, I am grateful for...

1.

2.

3.

Intention: Today, my intention is...

Committed Action: Today, the actions I will take to manifest my goals, dreams, and intentions are...

Date:

Gratitudes: Today, I am grateful for...

1.

2.

3.

Intention: Today, my intention is...

Committed Action: Today, the actions I will take to manifest my goals, dreams, and intentions are...

Date:

Gratitudes: Today, I am grateful for...

1.

2.

3.

Intention: Today, my intention is...

Committed Action: Today, the actions I will take to manifest my goals, dreams, and intentions are...

Date:

Gratitudes: Today, I am grateful for...

1.

2.

3.

Intention: Today, my intention is...

Committed Action: Today, the actions I will take to manifest my goals, dreams, and intentions are...

Date:

Gratitudes: Today, I am grateful for...

1.

2.

3.

Intention: Today, my intention is...

Committed Action: Today, the actions I will take to manifest my goals, dreams, and intentions are...

Date:

Gratitudes: Today, I am grateful for...

1.

2.

3.

Intention: Today, my intention is...

Committed Action: Today, the actions I will take to manifest my goals, dreams, and intentions are...

Date:

Gratitudes: Today, I am grateful for...

1.

2.

3.

Intention: Today, my intention is...

Committed Action: Today, the actions I will take to manifest my goals, dreams, and intentions are...

Date:

Gratitudes: Today, I am grateful for…

1.

2.

3.

Intention: Today, my intention is…

Committed Action: Today, the actions I will take to manifest my goals, dreams, and intentions are…

Date:

Gratitudes: Today, I am grateful for...

1.

2.

3.

Intention: Today, my intention is...

Committed Action: Today, the actions I will take to manifest my goals, dreams, and intentions are...

Date:

Gratitudes: Today, I am grateful for...

1.

2.

3.

Intention: Today, my intention is...

Committed Action: Today, the actions I will take to manifest my goals, dreams, and intentions are...

Date:

Gratitudes: Today, I am grateful for...

1.

2.

3.

Intention: Today, my intention is...

Committed Action: Today, the actions I will take to manifest my goals, dreams, and intentions are...

Date:

Gratitudes: Today, I am grateful for...

1.

2.

3.

Intention: Today, my intention is...

Committed Action: Today, the actions I will take to manifest my goals, dreams, and intentions are...

Date:

Gratitudes: Today, I am grateful for...

1.

2.

3.

Intention: Today, my intention is...

Committed Action: Today, the actions I will take to manifest my goals, dreams, and intentions are...

Date:

Gratitudes: Today, I am grateful for...

1.

2.

3.

Intention: Today, my intention is...

Committed Action: Today, the actions I will take to manifest my goals, dreams, and intentions are...

Date:

Gratitudes: Today, I am grateful for...

1.

2.

3.

Intention: Today, my intention is...

Committed Action: Today, the actions I will take to manifest my goals, dreams, and intentions are...

Date:

Gratitudes: Today, I am grateful for...

1.

2.

3.

Intention: Today, my intention is...

Committed Action: Today, the actions I will take to manifest my goals, dreams, and intentions are...

Date:

Gratitudes: Today, I am grateful for…

1.

2.

3.

Intention: Today, my intention is…

Committed Action: Today, the actions I will take to manifest my goals, dreams, and intentions are…

Date:

Gratitudes: Today, I am grateful for...

1.

2.

3.

Intention: Today, my intention is...

Committed Action: Today, the actions I will take to manifest my goals, dreams, and intentions are...

Date:

Gratitudes: Today, I am grateful for...

1.

2.

3.

Intention: Today, my intention is...

Committed Action: Today, the actions I will take to manifest my goals, dreams, and intentions are...

Date:

Gratitudes: Today, I am grateful for...

1.

2.

3.

Intention: Today, my intention is...

Committed Action: Today, the actions I will take to manifest my goals, dreams, and intentions are...

Date:

Gratitudes: Today, I am grateful for...

1.

2.

3.

Intention: Today, my intention is...

Committed Action: Today, the actions I will take to manifest my goals, dreams, and intentions are...

Date:

Gratitudes: Today, I am grateful for...

1.

2.

3.

Intention: Today, my intention is...

Committed Action: Today, the actions I will take to manifest my goals, dreams, and intentions are...

Date:

Gratitudes: Today, I am grateful for...

1.

2.

3.

Intention: Today, my intention is...

Committed Action: Today, the actions I will take to manifest my goals, dreams, and intentions are...

Date:

Gratitudes: Today, I am grateful for...

1.

2.

3.

Intention: Today, my intention is...

Committed Action: Today, the actions I will take to manifest my goals, dreams, and intentions are...

Date:

Gratitudes: Today, I am grateful for...

1.

2.

3.

Intention: Today, my intention is...

Committed Action: Today, the actions I will take to manifest my goals, dreams, and intentions are...

Date:

Gratitudes: Today, I am grateful for...

1.

2.

3.

Intention: Today, my intention is...

Committed Action: Today, the actions I will take to manifest my goals, dreams, and intentions are...

Date:

Gratitudes: Today, I am grateful for...

1.

2.

3.

Intention: Today, my intention is...

Committed Action: Today, the actions I will take to manifest my goals, dreams, and intentions are...

Date:

Gratitudes: Today, I am grateful for...

1.

2.

3.

Intention: Today, my intention is...

Committed Action: Today, the actions I will take to manifest my goals, dreams, and intentions are...

Date:

Gratitudes: Today, I am grateful for...

1.

2.

3.

Intention: Today, my intention is...

Committed Action: Today, the actions I will take to manifest my goals, dreams, and intentions are...

Date:

Gratitudes: Today, I am grateful for...

1.

2.

3.

Intention: Today, my intention is...

Committed Action: Today, the actions I will take to manifest my goals, dreams, and intentions are...

Date:

Gratitudes: Today, I am grateful for...

1.

2.

3.

Intention: Today, my intention is...

Committed Action: Today, the actions I will take to manifest my goals, dreams, and intentions are...

Date:

Gratitudes: Today, I am grateful for...

1.

2.

3.

Intention: Today, my intention is...

Committed Action: Today, the actions I will take to manifest my goals, dreams, and intentions are...

Date:

Gratitudes: Today, I am grateful for...

1.

2.

3.

Intention: Today, my intention is...

Committed Action: Today, the actions I will take to manifest my goals, dreams, and intentions are...

Date:

Gratitudes: Today, I am grateful for...

1.

2.

3.

Intention: Today, my intention is...

Committed Action: Today, the actions I will take to manifest my goals, dreams, and intentions are...

Date:

Gratitudes: Today, I am grateful for...

1.

2.

3.

Intention: Today, my intention is...

Committed Action: Today, the actions I will take to manifest my goals, dreams, and intentions are...

Date:

Gratitudes: Today, I am grateful for...

1.

2.

3.

Intention: Today, my intention is...

Committed Action: Today, the actions I will take to manifest my goals, dreams, and intentions are...

Date:

Gratitudes: Today, I am grateful for...

1.

2.

3.

Intention: Today, my intention is...

Committed Action: Today, the actions I will take to manifest my goals, dreams, and intentions are...

Date:

Gratitudes: Today, I am grateful for...

1.

2.

3.

Intention: Today, my intention is...

Committed Action: Today, the actions I will take to manifest my goals, dreams, and intentions are...

Date:

Gratitudes: Today, I am grateful for...

1.

2.

3.

Intention: Today, my intention is...

Committed Action: Today, the actions I will take to manifest my goals, dreams, and intentions are...

Date:

Gratitudes: Today, I am grateful for...

1.

2.

3.

Intention: Today, my intention is...

Committed Action: Today, the actions I will take to manifest my goals, dreams, and intentions are...

Date:

Gratitudes: Today, I am grateful for...

1.

2.

3.

Intention: Today, my intention is...

Committed Action: Today, the actions I will take to manifest my goals, dreams, and intentions are...

Date:

Gratitudes: Today, I am grateful for...

1.

2.

3.

Intention: Today, my intention is...

Committed Action: Today, the actions I will take to manifest my goals, dreams, and intentions are...

Date:

Gratitudes: Today, I am grateful for...

1.

2.

3.

Intention: Today, my intention is...

Committed Action: Today, the actions I will take to manifest my goals, dreams, and intentions are...

Date:

Gratitudes: Today, I am grateful for...

1.

2.

3.

Intention: Today, my intention is...

Committed Action: Today, the actions I will take to manifest my goals, dreams, and intentions are...

Date:

Gratitudes: Today, I am grateful for...

1.

2.

3.

Intention: Today, my intention is...

Committed Action: Today, the actions I will take to manifest my goals, dreams, and intentions are...

Date:

Gratitudes: Today, I am grateful for...

1.

2.

3.

Intention: Today, my intention is...

Committed Action: Today, the actions I will take to manifest my goals, dreams, and intentions are...

Date:

Gratitudes: Today, I am grateful for...

1.

2.

3.

Intention: Today, my intention is...

Committed Action: Today, the actions I will take to manifest my goals, dreams, and intentions are...

Date:

Gratitudes: Today, I am grateful for...

1.

2.

3.

Intention: Today, my intention is...

Committed Action: Today, the actions I will take to manifest my goals, dreams, and intentions are...

Date:

Gratitudes: Today, I am grateful for...

1.

2.

3.

Intention: Today, my intention is...

Committed Action: Today, the actions I will take to manifest my goals, dreams, and intentions are...

Date:

Gratitudes: Today, I am grateful for...

1.

2.

3.

Intention: Today, my intention is...

Committed Action: Today, the actions I will take to manifest my goals, dreams, and intentions are...

Date:

Gratitudes: Today, I am grateful for...

1.

2.

3.

Intention: Today, my intention is...

Committed Action: Today, the actions I will take to manifest my goals, dreams, and intentions are...

Date:

Gratitudes: Today, I am grateful for...

1.

2.

3.

Intention: Today, my intention is...

Committed Action: Today, the actions I will take to manifest my goals, dreams, and intentions are...

Date:

Gratitudes: Today, I am grateful for...

1.

2.

3.

Intention: Today, my intention is...

Committed Action: Today, the actions I will take to manifest my goals, dreams, and intentions are...

Date:

Gratitudes: Today, I am grateful for...

1.

2.

3.

Intention: Today, my intention is...

Committed Action: Today, the actions I will take to manifest my goals, dreams, and intentions are...

Date:

Gratitudes: Today, I am grateful for...

1.

2.

3.

Intention: Today, my intention is...

Committed Action: Today, the actions I will take to manifest my goals, dreams, and intentions are...

Date:

Gratitudes: Today, I am grateful for...

1.

2.

3.

Intention: Today, my intention is...

Committed Action: Today, the actions I will take to manifest my goals, dreams, and intentions are...

Date:

Gratitudes: Today, I am grateful for...

1.

2.

3.

Intention: Today, my intention is...

Committed Action: Today, the actions I will take to manifest my goals, dreams, and intentions are...

Date:

Gratitudes: Today, I am grateful for...

1.

2.

3.

Intention: Today, my intention is...

Committed Action: Today, the actions I will take to manifest my goals, dreams, and intentions are...

Date:

Gratitudes: Today, I am grateful for...

1.

2.

3.

Intention: Today, my intention is...

Committed Action: Today, the actions I will take to manifest my goals, dreams, and intentions are...

Date:

Gratitudes: Today, I am grateful for...

1.

2.

3.

Intention: Today, my intention is...

Committed Action: Today, the actions I will take to manifest my goals, dreams, and intentions are...

Date:

Gratitudes: Today, I am grateful for...

1.

2.

3.

Intention: Today, my intention is...

Committed Action: Today, the actions I will take to manifest my goals, dreams, and intentions are...

Date:

Gratitudes: Today, I am grateful for...

1.

2.

3.

Intention: Today, my intention is...

Committed Action: Today, the actions I will take to manifest my goals, dreams, and intentions are...

Date:

Gratitudes: Today, I am grateful for...

1.

2.

3.

Intention: Today, my intention is...

Committed Action: Today, the actions I will take to manifest my goals, dreams, and intentions are...

Date:

Gratitudes: Today, I am grateful for...

1.

2.

3.

Intention: Today, my intention is...

Committed Action: Today, the actions I will take to manifest my goals, dreams, and intentions are...

Date:

Gratitudes: Today, I am grateful for...

1.

2.

3.

Intention: Today, my intention is...

Committed Action: Today, the actions I will take to manifest my goals, dreams, and intentions are...

Date:

Gratitudes: Today, I am grateful for...

1.

2.

3.

Intention: Today, my intention is...

Committed Action: Today, the actions I will take to manifest my goals, dreams, and intentions are...

Date:

Gratitudes: Today, I am grateful for...

1.

2.

3.

Intention: Today, my intention is...

Committed Action: Today, the actions I will take to manifest my goals, dreams, and intentions are...

Date:

Gratitudes: Today, I am grateful for...

1.

2.

3.

Intention: Today, my intention is...

Committed Action: Today, the actions I will take to manifest my goals, dreams, and intentions are...

Date:

Gratitudes: Today, I am grateful for...

1.

2.

3.

Intention: Today, my intention is...

Committed Action: Today, the actions I will take to manifest my goals, dreams, and intentions are...

Date:

Gratitudes: Today, I am grateful for...

1.

2.

3.

Intention: Today, my intention is...

Committed Action: Today, the actions I will take to manifest my goals, dreams, and intentions are...

Date:

Gratitudes: Today, I am grateful for...

1.

2.

3.

Intention: Today, my intention is...

Committed Action: Today, the actions I will take to manifest my goals, dreams, and intentions are...

Date:

Gratitudes: Today, I am grateful for...

1.

2.

3.

Intention: Today, my intention is...

Committed Action: Today, the actions I will take to manifest my goals, dreams, and intentions are...

Date:

Gratitudes: Today, I am grateful for...

1.

2.

3.

Intention: Today, my intention is...

Committed Action: Today, the actions I will take to manifest my goals, dreams, and intentions are...

Date:

Gratitudes: Today, I am grateful for...

1.

2.

3.

Intention: Today, my intention is...

Committed Action: Today, the actions I will take to manifest my goals, dreams, and intentions are...

Date:

Gratitudes: Today, I am grateful for...

1.

2.

3.

Intention: Today, my intention is...

Committed Action: Today, the actions I will take to manifest my goals, dreams, and intentions are...

Date:

Gratitudes: Today, I am grateful for...

1.

2.

3.

Intention: Today, my intention is...

Committed Action: Today, the actions I will take to manifest my goals, dreams, and intentions are...

Date:

Gratitudes: Today, I am grateful for...

1.

2.

3.

Intention: Today, my intention is...

Committed Action: Today, the actions I will take to manifest my goals, dreams, and intentions are...

Date:

Gratitudes: Today, I am grateful for...

1.

2.

3.

Intention: Today, my intention is...

Committed Action: Today, the actions I will take to manifest my goals, dreams, and intentions are...

Date:

Gratitudes: Today, I am grateful for...

1.

2.

3.

Intention: Today, my intention is...

Committed Action: Today, the actions I will take to manifest my goals, dreams, and intentions are...

Date:

Gratitudes: Today, I am grateful for...

1.

2.

3.

Intention: Today, my intention is...

Committed Action: Today, the actions I will take to manifest my goals, dreams, and intentions are...

Date:

Gratitudes: Today, I am grateful for...

1.

2.

3.

Intention: Today, my intention is...

Committed Action: Today, the actions I will take to manifest my goals, dreams, and intentions are...

Date:

Gratitudes: Today, I am grateful for...

1.

2.

3.

Intention: Today, my intention is...

Committed Action: Today, the actions I will take to manifest my goals, dreams, and intentions are...

Date:

Gratitudes: Today, I am grateful for...

1.

2.

3.

Intention: Today, my intention is...

Committed Action: Today, the actions I will take to manifest my goals, dreams, and intentions are...

Date:

Gratitudes: Today, I am grateful for…

1.

2.

3.

Intention: Today, my intention is…

Committed Action: Today, the actions I will take to manifest my goals, dreams, and intentions are…

Date:

Gratitudes: Today, I am grateful for...

1.

2.

3.

Intention: Today, my intention is...

Committed Action: Today, the actions I will take to manifest my goals, dreams, and intentions are...

Date:

Gratitudes: Today, I am grateful for...

1.

2.

3.

Intention: Today, my intention is...

Committed Action: Today, the actions I will take to manifest my goals, dreams, and intentions are...

Date:

Gratitudes: Today, I am grateful for...

1.

2.

3.

Intention: Today, my intention is...

Committed Action: Today, the actions I will take to manifest my goals, dreams, and intentions are...

Date:

Gratitudes: Today, I am grateful for...

1.

2.

3.

Intention: Today, my intention is...

Committed Action: Today, the actions I will take to manifest my goals, dreams, and intentions are...

Date:

Gratitudes: Today, I am grateful for...

1.

2.

3.

Intention: Today, my intention is...

Committed Action: Today, the actions I will take to manifest my goals, dreams, and intentions are...

Date:

Gratitudes: Today, I am grateful for...

1.

2.

3.

Intention: Today, my intention is...

Committed Action: Today, the actions I will take to manifest my goals, dreams, and intentions are...

Date:

Gratitudes: Today, I am grateful for...

1.

2.

3.

Intention: Today, my intention is...

Committed Action: Today, the actions I will take to manifest my goals, dreams, and intentions are...

Date:

Gratitudes: Today, I am grateful for...

1.

2.

3.

Intention: Today, my intention is...

Committed Action: Today, the actions I will take to manifest my goals, dreams, and intentions are...

Date:

Gratitudes: Today, I am grateful for...

1.

2.

3.

Intention: Today, my intention is...

Committed Action: Today, the actions I will take to manifest my goals, dreams, and intentions are...

Date:

Gratitudes: Today, I am grateful for...

1.

2.

3.

Intention: Today, my intention is...

Committed Action: Today, the actions I will take to manifest my goals, dreams, and intentions are...

Date:

Gratitudes: Today, I am grateful for...

1.

2.

3.

Intention: Today, my intention is...

Committed Action: Today, the actions I will take to manifest my goals, dreams, and intentions are...

Date:

Gratitudes: Today, I am grateful for...

1.

2.

3.

Intention: Today, my intention is...

Committed Action: Today, the actions I will take to manifest my goals, dreams, and intentions are...

Date:

Gratitudes: Today, I am grateful for...

1.

2.

3.

Intention: Today, my intention is...

Committed Action: Today, the actions I will take to manifest my goals, dreams, and intentions are...

Date:

Gratitudes: Today, I am grateful for...

1.

2.

3.

Intention: Today, my intention is...

Committed Action: Today, the actions I will take to manifest my goals, dreams, and intentions are...

Date:

Gratitudes: Today, I am grateful for...

1.

2.

3.

Intention: Today, my intention is...

Committed Action: Today, the actions I will take to manifest my goals, dreams, and intentions are...

Date:

Gratitudes: Today, I am grateful for…

1.

2.

3.

Intention: Today, my intention is…

Committed Action: Today, the actions I will take to manifest my goals, dreams, and intentions are…

Date:

Gratitudes: Today, I am grateful for...

1.

2.

3.

Intention: Today, my intention is...

Committed Action: Today, the actions I will take to manifest my goals, dreams, and intentions are...

Date:

Gratitudes: Today, I am grateful for...

1.

2.

3.

Intention: Today, my intention is...

Committed Action: Today, the actions I will take to manifest my goals, dreams, and intentions are...

Date:

Gratitudes: Today, I am grateful for...

1.

2.

3.

Intention: Today, my intention is...

Committed Action: Today, the actions I will take to manifest my goals, dreams, and intentions are...

Date:

Gratitudes: Today, I am grateful for...

1.

2.

3.

Intention: Today, my intention is...

Committed Action: Today, the actions I will take to manifest my goals, dreams, and intentions are...

Date:

Gratitudes: Today, I am grateful for...

1.

2.

3.

Intention: Today, my intention is...

Committed Action: Today, the actions I will take to manifest my goals, dreams, and intentions are...

Date:

Gratitudes: Today, I am grateful for...

1.

2.

3.

Intention: Today, my intention is...

Committed Action: Today, the actions I will take to manifest my goals, dreams, and intentions are...

Date:

Gratitudes: Today, I am grateful for...

1.

2.

3.

Intention: Today, my intention is...

Committed Action: Today, the actions I will take to manifest my goals, dreams, and intentions are...

Date:

Gratitudes: Today, I am grateful for...

1.

2.

3.

Intention: Today, my intention is...

Committed Action: Today, the actions I will take to manifest my goals, dreams, and intentions are...

Date:

Gratitudes: Today, I am grateful for...

1.

2.

3.

Intention: Today, my intention is...

Committed Action: Today, the actions I will take to manifest my goals, dreams, and intentions are...

Date:

Gratitudes: Today, I am grateful for...

1.

2.

3.

Intention: Today, my intention is...

Committed Action: Today, the actions I will take to manifest my goals, dreams, and intentions are...

Date:

Gratitudes: Today, I am grateful for...

1.

2.

3.

Intention: Today, my intention is...

Committed Action: Today, the actions I will take to manifest my goals, dreams, and intentions are...

Date:

Gratitudes: Today, I am grateful for...

1.

2.

3.

Intention: Today, my intention is...

Committed Action: Today, the actions I will take to manifest my goals, dreams, and intentions are...

Date:

Gratitudes: Today, I am grateful for...

1.

2.

3.

Intention: Today, my intention is...

Committed Action: Today, the actions I will take to manifest my goals, dreams, and intentions are...

Date:

Gratitudes: Today, I am grateful for...

1.

2.

3.

Intention: Today, my intention is...

Committed Action: Today, the actions I will take to manifest my goals, dreams, and intentions are...

Date:

Gratitudes: Today, I am grateful for...

1.

2.

3.

Intention: Today, my intention is...

Committed Action: Today, the actions I will take to manifest my goals, dreams, and intentions are...

Date:

Gratitudes: Today, I am grateful for…

1.

2.

3.

Intention: Today, my intention is…

Committed Action: Today, the actions I will take to manifest my goals, dreams, and intentions are…

Date:

Gratitudes: Today, I am grateful for...

1.

2.

3.

Intention: Today, my intention is...

Committed Action: Today, the actions I will take to manifest my goals, dreams, and intentions are...

Date:

Gratitudes: Today, I am grateful for...

1.

2.

3.

Intention: Today, my intention is...

Committed Action: Today, the actions I will take to manifest my goals, dreams, and intentions are...

Date:

Gratitudes: Today, I am grateful for...

1.

2.

3.

Intention: Today, my intention is...

Committed Action: Today, the actions I will take to manifest my goals, dreams, and intentions are...

Date:

Gratitudes: Today, I am grateful for...

1.

2.

3.

Intention: Today, my intention is...

Committed Action: Today, the actions I will take to manifest my goals, dreams, and intentions are...

Date:

Gratitudes: Today, I am grateful for...

1.

2.

3.

Intention: Today, my intention is...

Committed Action: Today, the actions I will take to manifest my goals, dreams, and intentions are...

Date:

Gratitudes: Today, I am grateful for...

1.

2.

3.

Intention: Today, my intention is...

Committed Action: Today, the actions I will take to manifest my goals, dreams, and intentions are...

Date:

Gratitudes: Today, I am grateful for...

1.

2.

3.

Intention: Today, my intention is...

Committed Action: Today, the actions I will take to manifest my goals, dreams, and intentions are...

Date:

Gratitudes: Today, I am grateful for...

1.

2.

3.

Intention: Today, my intention is...

Committed Action: Today, the actions I will take to manifest my goals, dreams, and intentions are...

Date:

Gratitudes: Today, I am grateful for...

1.

2.

3.

Intention: Today, my intention is...

Committed Action: Today, the actions I will take to manifest my goals, dreams, and intentions are...

Date:

Gratitudes: Today, I am grateful for...

1.

2.

3.

Intention: Today, my intention is...

Committed Action: Today, the actions I will take to manifest my goals, dreams, and intentions are...

Date:

Gratitudes: Today, I am grateful for...

1.

2.

3.

Intention: Today, my intention is...

Committed Action: Today, the actions I will take to manifest my goals, dreams, and intentions are...

Date:

Gratitudes: Today, I am grateful for...

1.

2.

3.

Intention: Today, my intention is...

Committed Action: Today, the actions I will take to manifest my goals, dreams, and intentions are...

Date:

Gratitudes: Today, I am grateful for...

1.

2.

3.

Intention: Today, my intention is...

Committed Action: Today, the actions I will take to manifest my goals, dreams, and intentions are...

Date:

Gratitudes: Today, I am grateful for...

1.

2.

3.

Intention: Today, my intention is...

Committed Action: Today, the actions I will take to manifest my goals, dreams, and intentions are...

Date:

Gratitudes: Today, I am grateful for...

1.

2.

3.

Intention: Today, my intention is...

Committed Action: Today, the actions I will take to manifest my goals, dreams, and intentions are...

Date:

Gratitudes: Today, I am grateful for...

1.

2.

3.

Intention: Today, my intention is...

Committed Action: Today, the actions I will take to manifest my goals, dreams, and intentions are...

Date:

Gratitudes: Today, I am grateful for...

1.

2.

3.

Intention: Today, my intention is...

Committed Action: Today, the actions I will take to manifest my goals, dreams, and intentions are...

Date:

Gratitudes: Today, I am grateful for...

1.

2.

3.

Intention: Today, my intention is...

Committed Action: Today, the actions I will take to manifest my goals, dreams, and intentions are...

Date:

Gratitudes: Today, I am grateful for...

1.

2.

3.

Intention: Today, my intention is...

Committed Action: Today, the actions I will take to manifest my goals, dreams, and intentions are...

.

Date:

Gratitudes: Today, I am grateful for...

1.

2.

3.

Intention: Today, my intention is...

Committed Action: Today, the actions I will take to manifest my goals, dreams, and intentions are...

Date:

Gratitudes: Today, I am grateful for...

1.

2.

3.

Intention: Today, my intention is...

Committed Action: Today, the actions I will take to manifest my goals, dreams, and intentions are...

Date:

Gratitudes: Today, I am grateful for...

1.

2.

3.

Intention: Today, my intention is...

Committed Action: Today, the actions I will take to manifest my goals, dreams, and intentions are...

Date:

Gratitudes: Today, I am grateful for...

1.

2.

3.

Intention: Today, my intention is...

Committed Action: Today, the actions I will take to manifest my goals, dreams, and intentions are...

Date:

Gratitudes: Today, I am grateful for...

1.

2.

3.

Intention: Today, my intention is...

Committed Action: Today, the actions I will take to manifest my goals, dreams, and intentions are...

Date:

Gratitudes: Today, I am grateful for...

1.

2.

3.

Intention: Today, my intention is...

Committed Action: Today, the actions I will take to manifest my goals, dreams, and intentions are...

Date:

Gratitudes: Today, I am grateful for...

1.

2.

3.

Intention: Today, my intention is...

Committed Action: Today, the actions I will take to manifest my goals, dreams, and intentions are...